INTRODU

Welcome to Scotland ... Book

This handy guide will introduce you to the vibrant and unique dialect of Scotland. Whether you're a tourist, a new resident, or a language enthusiast, this book will help you navigate and enjoy Scottish expressions.

Purpose of the Book
Our goal is to make learning Scottish slang fun and easy. With this guide, you'll understand and use these colorful terms like a local.

How to Use This Book
The book is organized in an A-Z format for quick reference. Each entry includes:
- Word/Phrase: The slang term.
- Pronunciation: Phonetic spelling.
- Definition: Simple explanation.
- Example Sentence: Contextual usage.
- Explanation: Additional context.

Embrace the dialect and enjoy the wit and warmth of Scottish communication. Let's get started on this linguistic adventure!

A

AYE
(aɪ)

Definition

Yes

Example Sentence

"Are ye coming tae the pub the night?" "Aye, I'll be there."

Explanation

"Aye" is a common Scottish term for "yes."

AULD
(Oːld)

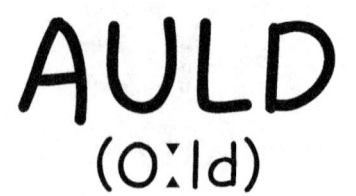

Definition

Old

Example Sentence

"That's an auld castle."

Explanation

"Auld" is the Scots word for "old," often used in phrases like "Auld Lang Syne."

AWFY
(ˈɔːfi)

Definition

Awful or very

Example Sentence

"It's awfy cold outside."

Explanation

"Awfy" can mean "awful" or be used to emphasize something, similar to "very."

AH DINNAE KEN
(əˈdIneI kɛn)

Definition

I don't know

Example Sentence

"Where's John?" "Ah dinnae ken."

Explanation

"Ah dinnae ken" means "I don't know" in Scots.

B

ABOOT
(ə'buːt)

Definition

About

Example Sentence

"What are ye talkin' aboot?"

Explanation

"Aboot" is the Scots pronunciation of "about."

BAIRN
(bɛərn)

Definition

Child

Example Sentence

"The bairn is playin' in the garden."

Explanation

"Bairn" is used in Scotland and Northern England to refer to a young child.

BLETHER
(ˈblɛðər)

Definition

Chat or gossip

Example Sentence

"Let's have a blether over a cup of tea."

Explanation

"Blether" means to have a casual conversation, often about trivial matters.

BONNIE
(ˈbɒni)

Definition

Beautiful or pretty

Example Sentence

"What a bonnie lass she is."

Explanation

"Bonnie" is used to describe someone or something that is attractive or pleasant.

BRAW
(Braw)

Definition

Fine or good

Example Sentence

"It's a braw day for a walk."

Explanation

"Braw" is used to describe something excellent or pleasing.

BAMPOT
(ˈbæmpɒt)

Definition

Fool or idiot

Example Sentence

"Don't be such a bampot!"

Explanation

"Bampot" is a playful or mildly derogatory term for someone acting foolishly.

C

CANNY
(ˈkæni)

Definition

Careful or shrewd

Example Sentence

"He's a canny lad, always thinking ahead."

Explanation

"Canny" is often used to describe someone who is prudent or has good judgment.

CHANCER
(ˈtʃænsər)

Definition

Opportunist or someone who takes risks

Example Sentence

"He's a real chancer, always looking for the next big thing."

Explanation

"Chancer" refers to someone who takes chances, often in a cheeky or unscrupulous manner.

CLAES
(kleIz)

Definition

Clothes

Example Sentence

"Put on your best claes for the party."

Explanation

"Claes" is the Scots word for clothes.

CLARTY
(ˈklɑːrti)

Definition

Dirty or messy

Example Sentence

"Your shoes are awfully clarty."

Explanation

"Clarty" is used to describe something that is grimy or soiled.

CRAIC
(kræk)

Definition
Fun, entertainment, or good conversation

Example Sentence
"The party was great craic."

Explanation
"Craic" (often spelled "crack") is originally Irish but widely used in Scotland to mean enjoyable social activity or conversation.

D

DINNAE
(ˈdɪnə)

Definition

Don't

Example Sentence

"Dinnae worry aboot it."

Explanation

A contraction of "do not," often used in conversational Scottish English.

DREICH
(driːx)

Definition
Dreary or gloomy, typically referring to weather

Example Sentence
"It's a dreich day outside."

Explanation
"Dreich" describes damp, cold, and unpleasant weather conditions.

DAFT
(dæft)

Definition

Silly or foolish

Example Sentence

"Don't be daft, that's a crazy idea."

Explanation

"Daft" is used to describe someone who is acting silly or nonsensical.

DOOK
(dʊk)

Definition

To dunk or immerse, often used for swimming

Example Sentence

"Fancy a dook in the loch?"

Explanation

"Dook" is commonly used to refer to taking a dip in water.

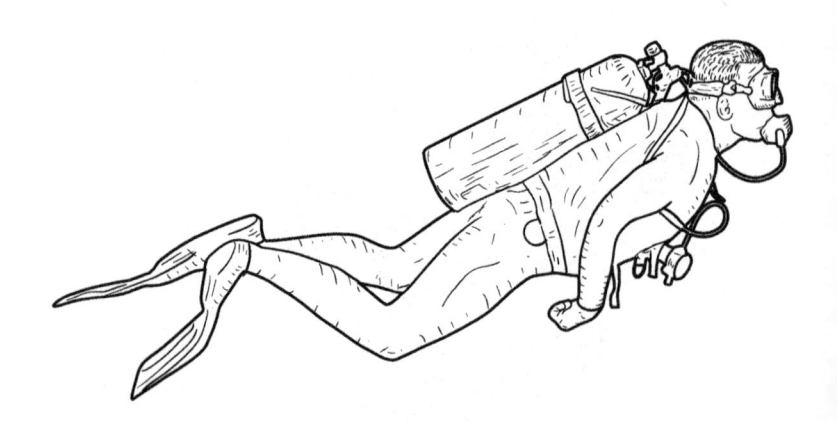

DREICH
(draɪ)

Definition
Dull, bleak, or dreary, often referring to weather

Example Sentence
"The weather's been awfully dreich this week."

Explanation
"Dreich" is a quintessential Scottish word to describe miserable weather.

&

EEJIT
(ˈiːdʒɪt)

Definition

Idiot or fool

Example Sentence

"Don't be such an eejit!"

Explanation

"Eejit" is a playful or mildly insulting term for someone behaving foolishly.

EEKSIE-PEEKSIE
(ˈiːksiˈpiːksi)

Definition

Even or equal

Example Sentence

"We'll split the bill eeksie-peeksie."

Explanation

"Eeksie-peeksie" means to divide something evenly between parties.

EH
(eI)

Definition

Used to seek agreement or clarification

Example Sentence

"Nice weather, eh?"

Explanation

Similar to the Canadian "eh," it's used at the end of a sentence to confirm understanding or agreement.

EMBRA
(ˈɛmbra)

Definition

Edinburgh (the capital city of Scotland)

Example Sentence

"I'm heading to Embra for the weekend."

Explanation

A colloquial term for Edinburgh, often used by locals.

EARN
(Ɛrn)

Definition

A Scottish term for an eagle

Example Sentence

"We saw an earn soaring above the hills."

Explanation

"Earn" is derived from Old Scots and refers specifically to eagles.

FANKLE
('fæŋkəl)

Definition

Tangle or mess

Example Sentence

"My shoelaces are in a fankle."

Explanation

"Fankle" is used to describe something that is tangled or in a state of confusion.

FASH
(fæʃ)

Definition

Worry or bother

Example Sentence

"Dinnae fash yersel' over it."

Explanation

"Fash" means to worry or trouble oneself about something.

FOOSTY
(ˈfuːsti)

Definition

Musty or stale

Example Sentence

"This bread's gone foosty."

Explanation

"Foosty" describes something that has become stale or developed a musty smell.

FITBA
(ˈfɪtbə)

Definition

Football (soccer)

Example Sentence

"Are ye watchin' the fitba the night?"

Explanation

"Fitba" is the Scots term for football, commonly used to refer to soccer.

FLIT
(flIt)

Definition

Move house or relocate

Example Sentence

"We're planning to flit next month."

Explanation

"Flit" means to move from one place to another, often used in the context of changing residence.

G

GALLUS
(ˈgæləs)

Definition

Bold or daring

Example Sentence

"He's a gallus lad, always up for a challenge."

Explanation

"Gallus" describes someone who is confident and maybe a bit cheeky.

GLAIKIT
(ˈɡleɪkɪt)

Definition

Stupid or foolish

Example Sentence

"Don't be so glaikit, pay attention."

Explanation

"Glaikit" is used to describe someone who is acting senseless or daft.

GREET
(griːt)

Definition

Cry or weep

Example Sentence

"The bairn's been greetin' all day."

Explanation

"Greet" means to cry or sob, often used in reference to children.

GUDDLE
(ˈgʌdəl)

Definition

Mess or muddle

Example Sentence

"What a guddle you've made of things!"

Explanation

"Guddle" describes a state of disorder or confusion.

GUISING
(ˈgaɪzɪŋ)

Definition

The Scottish tradition of children dressing up and going door-to-door at Halloween

Example Sentence

"The kids are out guising tonight."

Explanation

"Guising" is similar to trick-or-treating but with Scottish roots, where children perform a song, poem, or joke in exchange for treats.

H

HAUD
(hɔːd)

Definition

Hold

Example Sentence

"Haud on a minute, I'm coming."

Explanation

"Haud" is the Scots word for "hold," often used to mean "wait."

HAVERING
(ˈheɪvərɪŋ)

Definition

Talking nonsense

Example Sentence

"Stop havering and get to the point."

Explanation

"Havering" means to talk foolishly or without making much sense.

HEID
(hid)

Definition

Head

Example Sentence

"He's got a sore heid."

Explanation

"Heid" is the Scots word for "head."

HAME
(heIm)

Definition

Home

Example Sentence

"I'm going hame after work."

Explanation

"Hame" is the Scots word for "home."

I

I DINNAE KEN
(aɪ ˈdɪnə kɛn)

Definition
I don't know

Example Sentence
"Where's the nearest shop?" "I dinnae ken."

Explanation
A common Scots phrase meaning "I don't know."

INGIE
(ˈIndʒi)

Definition

A small piece or bit

Example Sentence

"Just give me an ingie of that cake."

Explanation

"Ingie" refers to a small portion of something.

ISNAE
(ˈIznə)

Definition

Isn't

Example Sentence

"He isnae coming to the party."

Explanation

A contraction of "is not," used in Scottish dialect.

ICKLE
(ˈɪkəl)

Definition

Little or small

Example Sentence

"Look at that ickle puppy!"

Explanation

"Ickle" is a term of endearment for something small or cute.

ITHER
(ˈɪðər)

Definition

Other

Example Sentence

"Do you have any ither suggestions?"

Explanation

"Ither" is the Scots word for "other."

J

JAG
(dʒæg)

Definition

Injection or shot

Example Sentence

"I'm off to the doctor for my flu jag."

Explanation

"Jag" is the Scottish term for a medical injection.

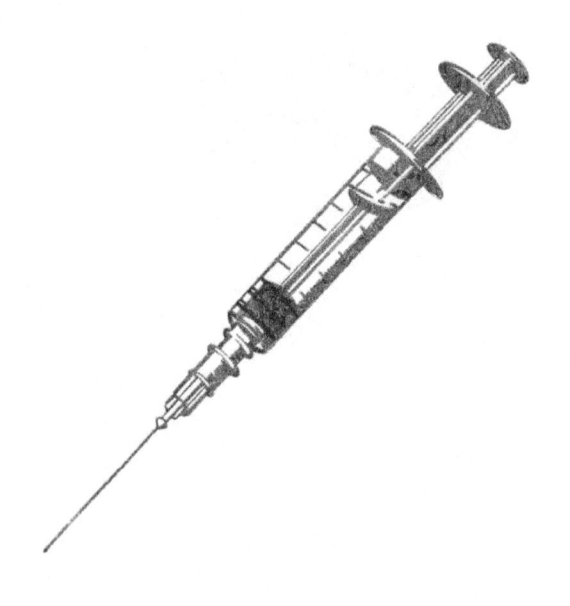

JINGS
(dʒɪŋz)

Definition

An exclamation of surprise or amazement

Example Sentence

"Jings, that was a close call!"

Explanation

"Jings" is an exclamation used to express shock or astonishment.

JOBBY
(ˈdʒɒbi)

Definition

Feces or poop

Example Sentence

"Mind you pick up the dog's jobby."

Explanation

"Jobby" is a slang term for excrement.

JEELIE
('dʒili)

Definition

Jelly or jam

Example Sentence

"I'd like some jeelie on my toast."

Explanation

"Jeelie" refers to fruit preserves, similar to jelly or jam.

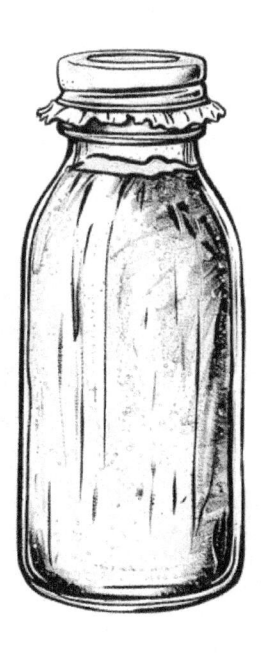

JOOK
(dʒʊk)

Definition

To duck or dodge

Example Sentence

"He had to jook to avoid the ball."

Explanation

"Jook" means to quickly move out of the way to avoid something.

K

KEN
(kɛn)

Definition

Know

Example Sentence

"Do ye ken what time it is?"

Explanation

"Ken" is a common Scots word meaning "know."

KEEK
(kiːk)

Definition
Peek or look quickly

Example Sentence
"Let's have a keek at the new café."

Explanation
"Keek" means to take a quick or secretive glance at something.

KILT
(kIlt)

Definition
A traditional Scottish garment

Example Sentence
"He wore a kilt to the wedding."

Explanation
"Kilt" is a knee-length skirt-like garment with pleats at the back, traditionally worn by Scottish men.

KNAP
(næp)

Definition
Bite or nibble

Example Sentence
"The dog gave a wee knap at the biscuit."

Explanation
"Knap" is a Scots term for taking a small bite or nibble.

KIRK
(kɜːrk)

Definition

Church

Example Sentence

"They're getting married in the kirk."

Explanation

"Kirk" is the Scots word for church.

L

LADDIE
(ˈlædi)

Definition

Boy or young man

Example Sentence

"The wee laddie is playing in the park."

Explanation

"Laddie" is used to refer to a boy or young man.

LASSIE
('læsi)

Definition

Girl or young woman

Example Sentence

"The lassie helped her mother with the shopping."

Explanation

"Lassie" is used to refer to a girl or young woman.

LUM
(lʌm)

Definition

Chimney

Example Sentence

"The smoke's coming out the lum."

Explanation

"Lum" is the Scots word for chimney.

LALDY
(ˈlældi)

Definition

With great energy or enthusiasm

Example Sentence

"He gave it laldy at the concert."

Explanation

"Laldy" means to do something with a lot of energy or effort.

LOUP
(luːp)

Definition

Leap or jump

Example Sentence

"He took a big loup over the stream."

Explanation

"Loup" is the Scots term for jump or leap.

M

MINGIN
(ˈmɪŋɪn)

Definition

Disgusting or dirty

Example Sentence

"This room is absolutely mingin."

Explanation

"Mingin" describes something that is very unpleasant or filthy.

MESSAGES
(ˈmɛsIdʒIz)

Definition

Groceries or shopping

Example Sentence

"I'm off to get the messages."

Explanation

In Scotland, "messages" refers to groceries or shopping items.

MUCKLE
(ˈmʌkəl)

Definition

Large or big

Example Sentence

"That's a muckle fish you've caught."

Explanation

"Muckle" is used to describe something large in size.

MOOTH
(muːθ)

Definition

Mouth

Example Sentence

"He's got a big mooth."

Explanation

"Mooth" is the Scots word for mouth.

MITHER
('mIðər)

Definition

To bother or pester

Example Sentence

"Stop mithering me while I'm working."

Explanation

"Mither" means to annoy or irritate someone by constantly bothering them.

N

NEB
(nɛb)

Definition

Nose

Example Sentence

"He's got a red neb from the cold."

Explanation

"Neb" is the Scots word for nose.

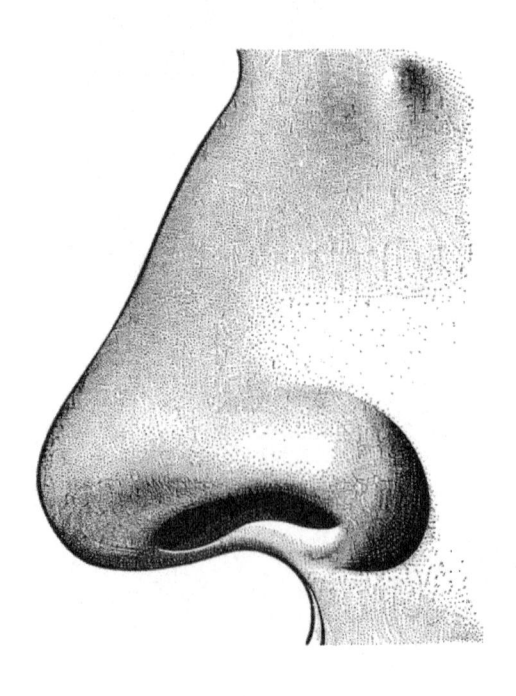

NEEP
(niːp)

Definition

Turnip

Example Sentence

"We're having haggis, neeps, and tatties for dinner."

Explanation

"Neep" refers to a turnip, often served with haggis.

NIPPIE SWEETIE
(ˈnIpi ˈswiːti)

Definition
A sharp-tongued or irritable person

Example Sentence
"She can be a real nippie sweetie when she's annoyed."

Explanation
"Nippie sweetie" describes someone who is easily irritated or sharp in their comments.

NATTER
(ˈnætər)

Definition

Chat or talk

Example Sentence

"We had a good natter over coffee."

Explanation

"Natter" means to have a casual conversation or chat.

O

OCH
(ɒx)

Definition

An exclamation of surprise, frustration, or resignation

Example Sentence

"Och, I forgot my keys!"

Explanation

"Och" is used to express a range of emotions, from mild annoyance to surprise.

OUTWITH
(aʊtˈwɪθ)

Definition
Outside of or beyond

Example Sentence
"This matter is outwith my control."

Explanation
"Outwith" means outside of or beyond something.

OXTER
(ˈɒkstər)

Definition

Armpit

Example Sentence

"Tuck it under your oxter."

Explanation

"Oxter" is the Scots word for armpit.

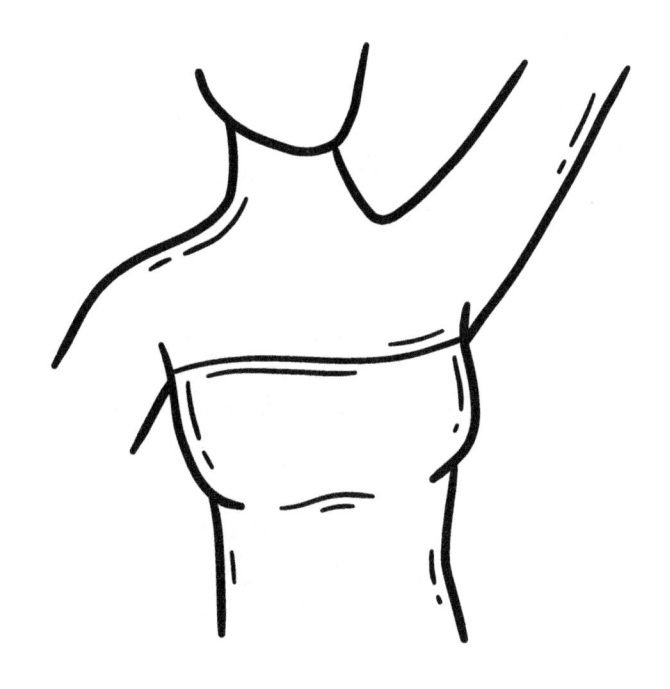

OWER
(ʌuər)

Definition
Over

Example Sentence
"He's ower the moon with his new job."

Explanation
"Ower" is the Scots pronunciation and spelling for "over."

ONY
(ˈɒni)

Definition

Any

Example Sentence

"Do you have ony sugar?"

Explanation

"Ony" is the Scots word for "any."

P

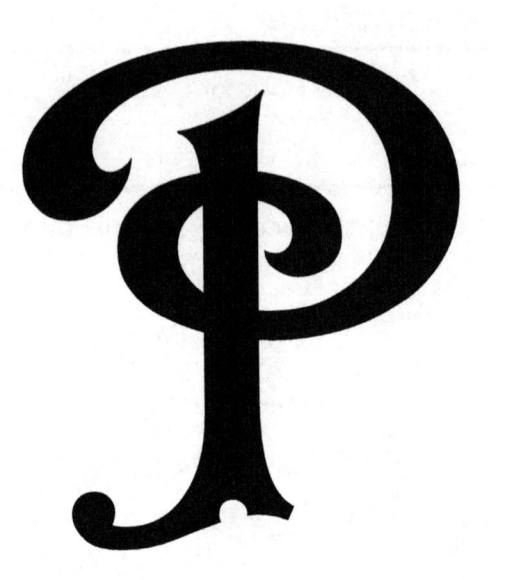

PEELY-WALLY
(ˈpiːli ˈwɔːli)

Definition

Pale or sickly looking

Example Sentence

"You're looking a bit peely-wally today."

Explanation

"Peely-wally" is used to describe someone who looks unwell or very pale.

PIECE
(piːs)

Definition

Sandwich

Example Sentence

"I've packed a piece for lunch."

Explanation

In Scotland, "piece" refers to a sandwich.

PUGGLED
(ˈpʌgəld)

Definition

Tired or exhausted

Example Sentence

"I'm feeling puggled after that run."

Explanation

"Puggled" means very tired or worn out.

PATTER
(ˈpætər)

Definition

Banter or chat

Example Sentence

"He's got great patter."

Explanation

"Patter" refers to the art of conversation, often involving witty or smooth talk.

PUGGIE
(ˈpʌɡi)

Definition

Slot machine or arcade game

Example Sentence

"He spent all his money on the puggie."

Explanation

"Puggie" is a Scots term for a slot machine or gaming machine found in arcades.

Q

QUINE
(kwIn)

Definition

Girl or young woman (mainly used in North East Scotland)

Example Sentence

"That quine is very clever."

Explanation

"Quine" is used in the Doric dialect to refer to a girl or young woman.

QUEER
(kwIər)

Definition
Strange or unusual

Example Sentence
"That's a queer looking building."

Explanation
"Queer" in Scots often means something strange or unusual, without the modern connotation related to sexual orientation.

QUATE
(kwet)

Definition

Quiet

Example Sentence

"The library is always quate."

Explanation

"Quate" is the Scots word for quiet.

R

REDD
(rɛd)

Definition
To tidy or clean

Example Sentence
"I need to redd up the kitchen before guests arrive."

Explanation
"Redd" means to clean or organize a space.

REEK
(riːk)

Definition

Smoke or strong smell

Example Sentence

"The fire's causing a lot of reek."

Explanation

"Reek" refers to smoke or a strong, often unpleasant smell.

ROON
(ruːn)

Definition

Round or around

Example Sentence

"Let's take a walk roon the park."

Explanation

"Roon" is the Scots pronunciation and spelling of "round" or "around."

RASH
(ræʃ)

Definition

Rush or hurry

Example Sentence

"Don't rash into making a decision."

Explanation

"Rash" means to hurry or do something quickly.

RICHT
(rIxt)

Definition

Right or correct

Example Sentence

"You were richt about the weather."

Explanation

"Richt" is the Scots word for "right" or "correct."

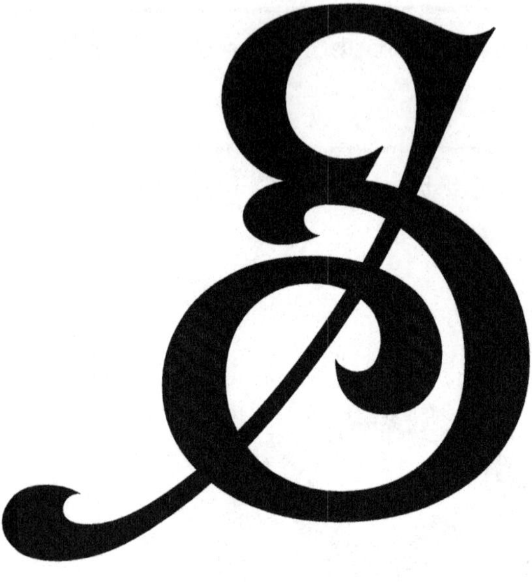

SASSENACH
(ˈsæsənæk)

Definition
An English person

Example Sentence
"He's a Sassenach from London."

Explanation
"Sassenach" is a term used by Scots to refer to someone from England, often in a playful or mildly derogatory manner.

SASSENACH
(ˈsæsənæk)

Definition

Fed up or disgusted

Example Sentence

"I'm scunnered with all this rain."

Explanation

"Scunnered" means being thoroughly fed up or disgusted with something.

SCRAN
(skræn)

Definition
Food

Example Sentence
"Let's get some scran; I'm starving."

Explanation
"Scran" is a slang term for food.

SHOOGLE
(ˈʃuːgəl)

Definition

Shake or wobble

Example Sentence

"The table's a bit shoogly."

Explanation

"Shoogle" means to shake or cause to wobble.

SKELP
(skɛlp)

Definition

Slap or smack

Example Sentence

"He gave him a skelp on the head."

Explanation

"Skelp" means to hit or slap someone, usually with the open hand.

T

TATTIE
(ˈtæti)

Definition

Potato

Example Sentence

"We're having haggis, neeps, and tatties for dinner."

Explanation

"Tattie" is the Scots word for potato.

TEUCHTER
(ˈtjuːxtər)

Definition

A person from the rural Highlands or islands of Scotland

Example Sentence

"He's a proud teuchter from the Isle of Skye."

Explanation

"Teuchter" is often used to describe someone from the rural areas of the Scottish Highlands.

THRAWN
(θrɔːn)

Definition

Stubborn or contrary

Example Sentence

"She's a thrawn lass, never gives up."

Explanation

"Thrawn" describes someone who is stubborn or obstinate.

TIDY
('taIdi)

Definition

Good or excellent

Example Sentence

"That's a tidy bit of work you've done."

Explanation

In Scottish slang, "tidy" can mean something that is neat, good, or well done.

TUMSHIE
(ˈtʌmʃi)

Definition

Turnip or an affectionate term for a fool

Example Sentence

"He carved a tumshie lantern for Halloween."

Explanation

"Tumshie" is the Scots word for turnip, and can also be used humorously to refer to someone who's acting foolishly.

UNCO
(ˈʌŋkoʊ)

Definition

Strange or unusual

Example Sentence

"That's an unco story ye're tellin'."

Explanation

"Unco" is used to describe something that is peculiar or out of the ordinary.

UGSOME
(ˈʌgsəm)

Definition

Disgusting or loathsome

Example Sentence

"The food looked ugsome, but it tasted fine."

Explanation

"Ugsome" is used to describe something that is particularly unpleasant or repulsive.

USQUEBAUGH
(ˈʌskwɪˌbɔː)

Definition

Whisky

Example Sentence

"A wee dram of usquebaugh warms ye up."

Explanation

"Usquebaugh" is an old term for whisky, derived from the Gaelic "uisge-beatha" meaning "water of life."

UPPY
(ˈʌpi)

Definition

Upwards or up

Example Sentence

"Throw the ball uppy to me."

Explanation

"Uppy" is a Scots term indicating an upward direction or movement.

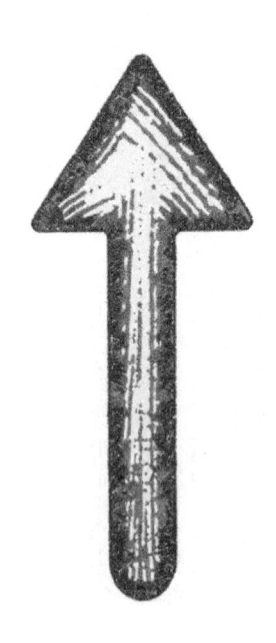

VERRA
(ˈvɛrə)

Definition

Very

Example Sentence

"It's verra cold today."

Explanation

"Verra" is the Scots word for "very."

VIM
(vIm)

Definition

Energy or enthusiasm

Example Sentence

"She tackled the job with vim and vigor."

Explanation

"Vim" means high energy or enthusiasm.

VOGIE
(ˈvoːgi)

Definition

Proud or vain

Example Sentence

"He's awfully vogie about his new car."

Explanation

"Vogie" describes someone who is overly proud or vain about something.

W

WEE
(wiː)

Definition
Small or little

Example Sentence
"He's just a wee lad."

Explanation
"Wee" is a common Scots word meaning small or little.

WAIN (OR WEAN)
(weIn)

Definition

Child

Example Sentence

"The wain is sleeping."

Explanation

"Wain" or "wean" is a term used in Scotland to refer to a child.

WABBIT
('wæbɪt)

Definition

Exhausted or tired

Example Sentence

"I'm feeling wabbit after that long walk."

Explanation

"Wabbit" means extremely tired or exhausted.

WUMMIN
(ˈwʊmɪn)

Definition

Woman

Example Sentence

"That wummin is very kind."

Explanation

"Wummin" is the Scots word for woman.

Y

YE
(jiː)

Definition

You

Example Sentence

"Are ye coming to the party?"

Explanation

"Ye" is the Scots word for "you."

YOKER
(ˈjoʊkər)

Definition

A resident of Yoker, a district in Glasgow

Example Sentence

"He's a proud Yoker."

Explanation

"Yoker" refers to someone from Yoker, a neighborhood in Glasgow.

YALDY
(ˈjaldi)

Definition

An exclamation of excitement or joy

Example Sentence

"We won the game, yaldy!"

Explanation

"Yaldy" is a Scottish exclamation used to express excitement or joy.

Z

ZEPHYR
(ˈzɛfər)

Definition
A gentle, mild breeze

Example Sentence
"A soft zephyr blew through the glen."

Explanation
"Zephyr" refers to a light, gentle breeze.

ZILCH
(zIltʃ)

Definition

Nothing or zero

Example Sentence

"There's zilch left in the cupboard."

Explanation

"Zilch" means nothing or zero, often used to emphasize the absence of anything.

CONCLUSION

This concludes our A-Z list of Scottish slang words and phrases. By familiarizing yourself with these terms, you'll gain a deeper understanding of Scottish culture and language. Whether you're traveling through Scotland, conversing with locals, or just having fun with words, we hope this phrase book serves as a handy and enjoyable guide.

Printed in Great Britain
by Amazon